DECODING DUST

B/awe
1st Edition
(official
version)
Sept.
2016

B.W. POWE

NeoPoiesisPress.com

NeoPoiesis Press, LLC

2775 Harbor Ave SW, Suite D, Seattle, WA 98126-2138
Inquiries: Info@NeoPoiesisPress.com
NeoPoiesisPress.com

Decoding Dust
ISBN 978-0-9903565-8-5 (pbk)
    1. Poetry. I. Powe, B.W.

LOC Number 2016905744

First Edition

Cover Design: Milo Duffin and Stephen Roxborough

Interior Symbol Design: Quade Zaban and Dale Winslow

Printed in the United States of America.

For Auxi

Wherever I walk without you
  I keep an open space beside me
     that is yours

Contents

"Espíritu sin nombre,
Indefinible esencia,
Yo vivo con la vida
Sin formas de la idea."

Gustavo Adolfo Bécquer
Rimas

Reader

Come quietly with me
into silent letters again

fellow falling cipher
in the alphabet marking

The shaman calls this page
an image skin

they'll call it
the dead tree medium

Come quietly with me
to decode the dust

in the speck
of a single word

how we could be breaking
breathing through

Sadhaka

I was in prison
unjustly jailed (I thought)

I asked for my freedom
The jailer refused

What was my crime I asked
Everything he said

Confused and angry
I wrote a letter to you

I received a lamp
a drawing made of lines and circles

a book with empty pages—some pencils—
a shawl and a cup for rain

these and the little food I was given
through the slot in the steel door

I read into the dark
reflected on the drawing

I wrote out shapes like letters
in the morning in your blank book

I prayed and kept warm by the lamp
and in the shawl then I fasted

drinking only from the small cup
filled with water that seeped into my cell

By day I became calm and happy
By night I drew and read more

Soon I saw between your lines
an open space and a silence

I saw the lines
become a shape like a map

Your map took me
to the crack in the floor

I scratched and dug there
By day I prayed and read

By night I learned how to dig
my way forward

slowly displacing the dirt
out the small barred window

When I came at last into
the sudden air the wind

the breath beyond the lines
the breathing behind the map

I knew the story lived in my hands
I stood up

What would I do now
with a soul

Dream-catching

Now I'll tell you a story an Ojibwa shaman told
about the time she was living her vision quest

I slept beside a bear in a cave of flowers
under blueberries and will-o'-the-wisps
the soil like a bed for our shudders
and I felt desire and my soul shook

I made love to the bear in the cave
in her embrace I touched the roots' pang
taboo words became seething sap
fusing me into the lasting tales of my nation

I rose in the morning mist with the bear
her child layered in ceremonial leaves
and petals born in secrets and sighs
I'd risen with my lover into the primeval other

Carrying the ancient mother on new skin
my bones and cells are branches and seeds
I rest and dream in my cabin home
after a meal of spelt bread and cedar tea

remembering
nuzzling at night
into her musky
storied fur

Blessing

She says "Cry out
cry out and write"

Epitaph

He faltered on the road
but surely stayed on it

Blessings

She is pregnant
with heart
and gives birth
to the earth

Dust

We were nameless
like you
until you shaped us

We chose exile
but remember the mysteries
coming out of that love

We defied the omens
but everything begins
in sacred expulsion

All crave a return

*

What's morning like in Eden
Without you—a withered hush
without us—the bare tree of knowing
no souls reflect in the slow streams

What's life like in the Garden
A dazzling cold brightness
fantastic heraldic creatures
silently graze on furloughed roots

Do once vibrant fields recall
The snake's tail—the questing story—
the heart that departed—our echoing—
voices lifted without angels' breath

Do Elohim dream does The Word ache
I say this softly my wife
you said it tenderly my husband
live our moment if only for a moment

What's midnight like in paradise
Darkness grieving—
finds nothing but words on stone
Worlds shifted in a kiss—Now on our own

Slaves

They fled through a breach in the wall—
The lovers shied free from their warrior abductors
and from then on they slept chained to one another
each night she would snap the silver bond around her ankle
then around his—and the lovers would sleep make love
sleep make love and lie together joined—the long strings
of metal rings wrapped round their ankles and feet
Come morning she would take the key from the pouch
she wore around her neck and she would unlock the chain
and they would set out travelling again

across fields through forests and by rivers and over fords
until it was time to rest and after move on

They came to entertain villagers and townsfolk
with songs poems dancing and recitations
about their escape from prison and their willing
sensual enslavement to one another

                              *

She practiced the tantric arts learning how to keep
her vagina so warm and moist
that he could sleep with his penis deep inside her
and they would rest at night in a temporary camp

chained and honeyed
mingling heat and erections
She loved his scent so much
she had to cleave to him this close

*

He practiced the tantric arts
to make his erections last
so he could stay hard inside her
They would sleep
like this without motion
just breathing
breathing in their chains
He loved her and her scent so much
he had to have her this close

*

The rumors spread about their passion
their spellbound possession of one another
and people in tent theatres lined aisles
to see them dance and recite
They shouted
"Show us your steel necklace
Show us how you sleep together"

The lovers would do so
All would be hushed
in amazement at their slavery
to touch and scent and adoration and flight

*

The lovers travelled and linked their necklace
and massaged one other with warming oils

ate slept bathed in the morning in the evening
danced and told stories about tantric arts and the art of chains
but no one truly listened
People preferred watching the slaves to love
and chattering about them over steaming drinks and cold wine

*

When the two came to die—young in their souls
old in their skin—they made the vow
to return in other forms
to flee through a breach in the wall and be together
They promised to manacle their hearts and bodies
to this ultimate intimacy

The two did reappear renamed—inseparable but remade—
in gardens under gaslight beside pyramids and towers
in mansions and ruined homes and cottages and on piers

by whipped-up seas swaying trees
in lobbies lounges chapels and libraries and dens
the chains a bracelet of pearls
a red silk chaplet a rosary of songs
a garland of charms a wedding band

in different incarnations

but always escaping to share the necklace of love
always deep inside one another always seeking
always saying to the world
We are slaves to the heart

*

The slaves searched and found and knew and renewed
each other and it is the quest that streams like a current
falling and following through time
in song-lines fables plays and diaries

in every poet and every poem
until

Route

At the crossing
you fell
and recognized
nothing

You asked for too much
you knew nothing
of this route
or that one

Here not a call
or a cry
not you not me
not even I

Resurrections

"Lazarus our friend is sleeping"

I was a spasm
awakening ashes
You burned me
your brand a betraying kiss
The sun scorches
trails vanish
in wind agitated sand

What do I want desert or words

      craving
        my grave
      beauty
        bliss
     to be
        done with it

What made you believe
I wanted to return

You haunt me
    with my tomb's
       rolled away stone

I haunt you
    like a spring
       out of synch

Liberation

Once the wind
tore us from tears
we followed the flood
by Zion's trees

and found our harps
floating on waves
while those of the air
summoned us here

Every captive land
a home a haven
No one a stranger
all destinations vital

Hallowed is this place
with no gates and walls

GeorgieY

October 1917
on the edge of Ashdown forest

*

I call myself GeorgieY instead of Hyde-Lees
my Scheherazade bewitching his amour—I conjured
a scherzo of enticements because I knew

I'd stop him from dallying into pale dainty arms
or with Maud or a pub-maid he'd call Leda
and never guess the daemons were mine

I'll outlive his eye—now he wakes up
between creamy silk sheets in the leisured Eros
of my budding boudoir

*

I moan
It's after midnight on our couch
I murmur
staring into violins and seeing the sound
I whisper
the phoenix flames again in a bed-lamp
unruly sprites invade county inns
armed heroes drive through nationalist nights
the new radio squawks psychic sensation

I sigh
giving you sockets of shock
I'm a white form mistress
a demure cloud in the wind

*

I say go on rave rage without armor
in the gyre of the ravishing years
it took to get your fantasies here

You told me how shades chase you
down the faerie funnels of our race
How awful for them to know you live

I tell you our phantoms will shroud
the Dublin crowd in a mystique haze
and declare the revelation of the age

*

(Softly I send along a wedding song

I need you to listen
wild old man of lust and vision

So I rhyme and dance
I speak in a trance

naked my enterprise
eloquent my surprise

Softly I send along a wedding song)

*

You call me Circe-Sybil
enchantress of the miraculous room

but I enamor you in my medium's breath
then you doze trusting in our marriage bed

A new spell will arouse apparitions and arias
spectral letters and coital ease

I'll toss my Rossetti hair
I'll let you call me Elizabeth or Jane

and you'll spurt your words onto our sheets
into my always virgin ears

while I know you'll cry a second coming
my GeorgieY

Dedication

Some invisible paths don't forget you
Some paths remember footsteps
Some invisible paths dream of you
Some paths wait for your next step

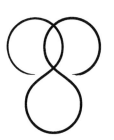

esoterica

if you invite destiny's star
there'll be a sundown then a sunrise place
a book of spells in braille

*

My children become gypsies
My dog quivers in his dreams
My mind reels in things

Home

"You're really a spiritual wannabe"
my seventeen-year-old daughter declared

That day she'd shaved her hair down
to a playful Pink-Annie-Lennox style
dyeing it platinum blond—it looked good

"Well it's not that hard to see" I said
"Best to keep it hidden" my son stated firmly

He'd grown a blond beard
his twin sister saying "*Sup omigod* you look
like Ryan Gosling in *The Notebook lol*"

So I make my trip (masked in fragments)
listening for the spirit

trying to speak the stranger heart
shaping the soul's ache
in the coming emanations—in prayer

Silence

Working late in my book-lined office at YorkU
I glanced up to see Marzena our college cleaning lady
stopping to gab at my open door

She was usually discreet and reserved
but that night she paused to share
a joke or two on her shift and I smiled

Until grief scraped her voice
and she told me of her son dead at seventeen
from a heart spasm one year ago to the day

"One moment he's here"
her Polish accent thickened her tone trembling
"And the next he's gone"

She cried out "Why are boys so silent
Why do they hide themselves
in video games"

I hadn't known about her devastating loss
and her pain made me stand and hug her
Marzena's sorrow knifing a hole in me—suddenly—

Possessed by a picture of teenagers
terrorized—tussled—wooed and cradled
by leeching wraiths a throbbing subliminal beat

our children withdrawn into windowless moods
sucked down into a livid gloom
doctors can't or won't name

that clamps onto their minds—
boys especially menaced in zones
of antsy sensitive fatigue

I saw them so plagued
by what—could we say—that they spend time
stringing their guitars in the dark

"He said nothing about his feelings" She was quiet
remote now "Nothing—The silence in our house"
She stared off "But—what can you do"

I sat back down and asked her why
she worked long hours in this brick maze
of corridors and deserted offices

She said "You find a place not so busy to work
a nice place where you feel good
and you do what you can"

She said she was once told
her name meant
like a dream

Lesson

Then my twins moved out
into university residence on the Monday
called Labour Day at the beginning
of the fall term

My daughter into one dorm called The Pond
My son into another called Calumet

And our home went quiet still
our dog Lucky poked first into one room
then another sniffing
the emptied spaces

What were my feelings
elation and sorrow
because I felt free
to invent new ways

because I missed them
our bond had been raw love
a muddled struggle through
too much

I honored their move
the time in this house
by planting two trees
in the stark back yard

A Glen-liven Linden for my daughter
A Green-mountain Maple for my son

Whoever comes after will surely know
children grew up here
during divorce and hungry hours

The cliché says "We give them
roots and wings"

and in their free flight into adulthood
(my God they were only seventeen
when they left)
they can gaze back at those trees

Today gray and stormy
the Linden and Maple have their first test
in a coarse blast of wind
and cool slanting rain

They're learning
how to bend

Teenagers

My kids over eighteen you say
you're wounded hard-pressed to heal
the sensational gouges we routed into you
from parental strife our lost hopes

careless cruelties and the deep strain
of living too impatiently—yet love haunts quickly
you glance up—from a light-soaked room
to a tree with numinous leaves

fluttering grace
in a wave of blue spectrum wind

You know sometimes our house has a pulse
restless uncanny even arrhythmic
but still beating
I see

baby twins both of you in your mother's arms
waving goodbye
and hello

tiny hands
clasping
unclasping

my happiness
at your welcome
and farewell

PG 18

"Parents should be seen, not heard"
God save my teenagers from my ignorance
save them from my authority and blind intentions
conserve in them the capacity for birth and rebirth
preserve their freedom from family
they may return someday if they wish

Keep their souls safe from their culture
and their overt teachers and preachers
keep them from over-praising their so-called betters
keep the scalding which inspires and estranges
may they find a guide to the tele-city ruckus
in the buffeting underworld 365-24-7

Let them nod in kind recognition
before they slip by or away
smile share a blessing or two then pass on
let them select their travel mates well
according to passion and a sweet faith in heaven
finding some way to be transparent and spare

Son

Carry this page
press it a faded leaf
in your wallet
or pocket

Carry it a token of love
found in the morning
in the ruts and grit
where you walk along with others

A keynote
A memento
A good luck charm
A word uttered from the other side of the wall

Carry this
fragment of our hearts
broken
so we may know

the blessing
between us
the peace
we deeply want

Elegy

"Come home" I said to my kids
"Lucky is dying"
Two strains of cancer ripped through him
He was straggling off to his cushion
groaning into sleep

Our dog hadn't eaten for days
the palliative Medicam wasn't helping
and he peed black blood on the carpet
his once shiny eyes now pleading

He taught me a lot
close to the end
he tried to play and make me smile
but he dug a hole under the porch
when I coaxed him out
he looked into me

and I knew it was time
the little collie who'd traipsed and jingled
on the forest path
who made us laugh at his antics
with squirrels and birds

Daughter you came and stayed
Son your quiet pained visit

Lucky died in my arms in the mourning room
at the vet's—after the quick injection

and I'd say a lot more
but this is all
I can manage

Incautious

She said "Leap before you look
the air is there to care
for you be imprudent

before the snares and coils
of protocol and prudence
the walls and shields

thicken and harden
the icon and shrine know
the leap is belief in the wind

let it sway
and dizzy your heart
leap before you look"

Inscribe

You said "Our gravestones should read
Why
did we never get close enough
to love"

Titles

This Book is a Person
This Book is a Tree

School of the Moon
On Heartland Maybe

Mystical Desperation
Communicating with Powers beyond the Human

For Rent—This Skin
Moonlight and Semen

Unconscious Explosion
Songs from a Submerged Cathedral

A Hatful of Nights
Dusted by Spectral Ash

Doves from Her Eyes
The Eternally Homeless Child

Where Meanings Aren't
Windmills Melting like Dali Clocks

The Night Can't Hurt Us
Portraits of the Sun

Shapeless Friends
Separate Seas

You're Made of Now
Comets from Paradise

Transcendence

You sleep on this shore
you wake on another

Your soul dreams in seas
your body rests in bed

Amoretti

On her FastLOve site the sexpert says

Revolutionary roads lead to group gropes
behind locked doors in any small Ontario town
wife swapping—swinging—threesomes—girl
on girl—boy on boy—voyeurs of pussy and cock

Baby the exurbia backwater awash with cum
and goosebumps—black whips and thigh-high boots
fuck-night and cocaine orgies in hot tubs
girls dressed like Place Pigalle whores

They zip up for Sunday brunch take a breather
slink back to corporate offices Monday
over coffees recall squirting and booty calls
the delicious skank and kink the golden shower

Boy O boy you don't know the unbridled Eros
secretly erupting in debauched dens
middle-class rocker lifestyles permission
given to raunch and roll

*

The micro-blogger tweets
then re-tweets

The brain is the new science mission my hyper-focus
neuron plasticity meaning malleability

The brain is the hard-code vibration
*We're moldable meat factories
this is the evolutionary voltage behind every selfie

**Sounds grandiloquent

You better believe it

***A word to the wise guy
cells
          it's all about cells

Set off dendrites
Excite axons
X-Ray the right/left hemispheres

****A feed to neo-cognitives everywhere

The neuro-cosmos is the turning point
where you must do MRIs

to not be
an idiot

*

*A church member cc'ing all
in her email*

While intellectuals
sit detached
locked into loneliness
studying theories and stats

exalted carols call
from Jerusalem's chapel
broken brethren cry
from their furnace depths

I see glistening baptisms
I hear sermons in tongues
Jesus is offering Eden
Love just for us

Bethlehem's star
fires the frontier in my heart
The Lord's holy holy touch
takes my willing hand

*

Fragments I found on slips of paper—
shambles
on my desk

I've passed by windows and churches at twilight
(are we all voyeurs and exhibitionists)
wondering what have I missed

What are the mysteries here
when I meditate and meander
in the blank of my evening

An Audi tilted—shaking—
three heads popped up inside
Two women and a man (I guessed)

Was it stolen
or (more likely) a rub and pull
Meet-Me-For-Sex romp

The Audi started up swinging off bouncing
zigzagging racing on
Was the team smiling

Where did I find this story
to revise and polish—I can't recall—
fumbling unprofitably over scrabbly notes

Abashed about longing for a unifying sign
I linger late in my kitchen looking for two doves
that perched lilting on the back yard fence

The doves sang with a strangely ecstatic tone—
so much energy—
only to sing

Morning light—
my heartbeat confession—room now—I hope
for more than I can see

Yearning

I was supposed to carry you
your flesh can hide the heart

I was supposed to feel you
your bones have caged your love

I was supposed to hear you
your skin shuttered your cry

I was supposed to meet you
your body won't let your soul out

I was supposed to hold you
what is it that stops love from leaping

my heart won't tear from its case
your distance burns up all the words

I was supposed to find passion here
I was supposed to carry you

Missing

It was the essential part
the line sputtered before nodding off
the image singed after the film's final credit
the echo after the last downbeat

The imperative slipped by
its imprint a track on fresh snow
moonlight purling on a pond's face
a drop of red wine left in the tall cup

After you left I wasn't the same
After your silence I kept hearing your voice
After you disappeared I imagined your return
After your call my heart sounded louder than before

wishing

this day
this moment
will be

brutally
gently

happy

lines

intimate

inarticulate

sight

of

tears

Remembrance

Here's a story my mother told me
in the early stages of her dementia
She was starting to unstitch and stitch the lines
of her past in a centre for chronic care

Censorship ruled the letters from the trenches
those World War One soldiers couldn't tell
their loved ones what they witnessed
or where they fought or what they thought

My English-lit high school teachers said
they wrote intimate notes to one another
but the censor blacked out the names
of the terrifying places and their suffering

He let his grammar and diction decay
his letters carried blatant errors
until he could write I'm *psalmwhere*
and the warden of words let it pass

She knew at last the location of hell
she found it on a map praying
Sommewhere he'd hear her
calling be safe my love be safe

Auguries

Can you listen to the shaman
Will you cross into oracular time

Can you follow into hospital wards
Will your mind skitter craving links

Can you slip between other dimensions
Will you travel without directions

*

I'm tallying up my dead
how many members of our family gone
one to cancer—my brother-in-law Paul
one to Alzheimer's—my aunt Myra

Two friends to accidents—DJ McKee and Joseph Amar
a musician and a painter—both gifted and avid
Teachers colleagues neighbors acquaintances
a well-respected peer a translator at YorkU

My mother dwindled into dementia
The phone zizzed—another one
in intensive care and I was tempted to say
inevitable things about gravity and ashes

Some of them young—in their 30s or 40s—
a few in their 60s and 80s
my address book filled with scribbled out
names and phone numbers

the words deceased passed on
scratched vaguely across them
I was getting woozy with vertigo
staring at the drill of blanks

*

Hospital Piece in Toronto

"Do you believe in Euthanasia"
my mother leaned out of her torpor
and listlessly asked me
"Why do you say that mom"
I said taken aback

She shrugged off my tone
her eyes yellowed blurring
and muttered "I do"
as if she was at a mysterious wedding
and told to give a stranger away

"What's that outside" she asked distracted
"What do you mean" I replied
"That" she said pointing
"You mean the sign"
"Yes what does it say"

"One way" I said
"Well—will I ever get well again—
I just saw my father your granddad
in the park he was strolling from heaven
smoking a cig" she said

The next minute we watched falling leaves
an orange leaf pressed to the window like a star
on a backdrop of clouds and drizzle
others exquisite yellow brown red gold
a still lush green one dancing

*

The shaman told me
in the Ojibwa magic traditions
they call dementia time-jumping
prophetic revelatory havened euphoric

shattering the triple moment
to let the wound of the present be
a crack through which zenith clarities
and confessions caper and confound

The shaman said nurturing death is
an illuminated passage
to the creator's dominion
time for celebrating the unknown

*

We launch ourselves towards dawning
un-harbored sky unanchored earth
séance realms where the dead tell us
their mornings are brighter than stars

*

In her urine stained bed my mother lay
gnarled up on one side
stretched out with wan stitches
down her blue-veined leg

And she was grouchy
confined with other patients in this sterilized room
she'd aged more than her eighty-four years in a week
From her cramped ache she moaned

rambling her words in scraps
saying "I'm in Camrose with my mom—"
We couldn't truly understand this
yet we shared her unstuck realities

Under the green light over her head
she seemed to daydream curtained off—
omnipresent TV voices intoning
editorial doom like too eager Jeremiahs—

She sipped apple juice
hand shaking on the paper cup
pale lips on white straw
juice drops falling like crumbs on her bedsheet

A nurse with a bleachy scent
bustling impatiently—maybe too tired
to be vulnerable to anyone's suffering—
became suddenly gentle with her
asking "Would you like a Tylenol 3"

My sister massaged our mother's hands
(None of us could think of what else to do)
She thanked her then mumbled "My dad's home"
And I recalled the shaman's smile—
how she'd renamed herself Raven—

She'd said "Lift the living veil of the eternal
and find the thriving yes in love
This time is hallowed
unadorned light"

Though I don't know if my family believed
in any thoughts of an extrasensory self
a transcendent third eye

*

Dream Piece

To whom do you speak
when you sleep

in your narrow bed
with ushering ghosts

You're made of streets
She's made of the sea

The shaman prays on dew
shape shifting she says

"The old is shedding skin
away from the new"

I hoped my mother would have more life
this reclusive woman unfazed by chaos
who'd thrived inside the hem of her reading
her children her piano and her husband

I hoped she'd find peace and grace
away from the ward's hygienic white
the correct protocol of doctors
the fluttery fear of my kindly dad

(they'd been married for 62 years)
the necessarily protective self-involvement
of my teenaged kids and the tender sad
look of my sister who'd spent so much time
outside surgery rooms—and my need to prattle

I'd hoped our mother would have the chance
to ease into air while we wrestled
with the cryptic awareness
the grudging unease of wanting
all this to end

I'd hoped her shrinking force
and body would yield to the imperial pride
of her often sarcastic tongue
("No dear that's not for you—"
"Christ dear sit still—")

At least her enveloping dementia
sometimes made her forget
where she was

("Why am I in the hospital—"
"Why can't you take me back—")

On the border of angels and the unforeseen
she'd begun to gabble with the irruptive dead
And I sensed how she could scar us
eternally spooking from beyond
if her soul leapt without forgiving

*

"Son my mother is telling me
I should be practicing the piano"

Days on she addressed the walls
abruptly time-splicing again

"I'm supposed to be playing
Mozart and Chopin

"But I can't because my cat is
prancing down the keys

"Maybe I should ask her to dance
and play a Nocturne for us"

My grandma dead since 1994
The cat's name long forgotten

"Your father has nothing now
When he comes to see me

he visits a wreck" she said
in a loving instant of lucid mercy

*

You opened the spare door
and went into your home
everything was bare

No one
lived there
not even you

*

Raven said "Your stirring soul
the higher self
made of ethereal steel
won't let everything die"

*

Virgin-Mobile Call Display
Green button on

My mom and I talked
about her hospital day
("It's predictable" she said sighing)
and of my dad's visit and my sister's

"O yes" she said startling me
with her brightening
"They came this morning"
her voice full of fondness

"We had such a good time together"
Only I found out later
they hadn't been there

Haggard—frazzled
they'd stayed home doing
laundry and chores
then fell to snoozing

We said we loved
every one truly
The red button off
led screen stating

(white light matter of fact)
our call's duration—2:38

*

Mother
A rose in dust
turns into leaves
at your touch

Mother
I'm trying to read you
to read
the dust

*

The shaman welcomed me to her Udora cabin
for a lunch of squash soup greens oranges and crusty bread
Outside blue-jays and cardinals chittered and pecked at feeders
Serene baby deer nibbled on grass

She said "Your mother has met many travelers
through mirages and miracles
She's travelling to the creator
through stories and memories

"Help her in her monastic ward
She's carrying the crystal beyond
receiving late-night messengers
the purveyors of her eventual peace

"Every lilac petal every oak leaf
every raindrop pool snowflake and dune

"They're all different original
both alpha and omega

"Every cuticle particle cell follicle
carries its own rebirth

"Remember her like that"

*

My mother furiously scratching out at us
baffled—stymied by her verbal salads
"What am I doing here—Who are you"
and Raven speaking of a doorway soul

the release into the flight
across the river and into the shades
where the dead share communion wafers
and wine goblets made of lilies

The shaman asked "Can you envision this
If you truly called on the creator
would you know what's the time
on your spiritual clock"

*

Street Piece in Stouffville

In my town today workers saw up trees
grinding branches of overgrown Maples
on our block—the truck's cogs and wheels
rev rumble with shimmying power

In garages my savvy neighbors—
shirt-sleeves rolled—devotedly restore cars and vans
In yards mothers breathlessly chase and coo
after scampering giddy kids

66

Life thrumming life scrabbling
life ratcheting up its emanations
life bivouacing and composing us
with laughter and shouts

*

My brother-in-law was disappearing
Could we grasp this

The convulsion of silence
in his blinking eyes
He jittered—gasping
in the fierce brace of the end

his ravaging too vast to know
like particles and quasars

Their home had turned quiet
though the rain on the roof drummed louder

And he was powerfully bare
in his departure
shy and hesitant
in his last murmuring

*

The shaman said "Be proud of them
and their dying

"They've added their shudder
to the world

"The creator made the willow and birch
the wolf the weed the owl and creek
the sparrow and rainbow the moon and meteor
his face and hers

"But your mother and brother-in-law
made beauty where there was none before

"They've helped to knit the world together
in the great weave of sympathy"

*

My sister sat at his bedside
listening
to his clotted breathing

She caressed his swollen face
and stroked his emaciated hands
kissing his eyelids

then she flurried off to the kitchen
to make vegetable soup
for her teenage son

She was a valiant watcher like a crier
in a medieval town set to announce
the news and dowse the lamps

Later she perched on her bed's edge
trying to relax preparing the next steps
when evening melded with exhaustion

and his soul soared
brushing her cheek with astral breath
he laughed lifting

his Aussie guffaw—"No worries mate"—
his sardonic presence leaving
he touched her hair with air

without her sensing or knowing it
gliding on he said
"Hey I'm okay now"

*

I shivered slightly in my bedroom
kilometers from their village Warkworth and their rural home
overlooking a broad wooded valley
maybe it was—a rainbow arch instant—light striking—

through a curtainless window a screen-door springing wide
turbulence from the shaman's words
expanding mystery a discovery of inter-dimensionalities
and my hectic imagining merging

with my sister's call
area codes 705 to 905

when I heard her quietly say
"He's—my husband's—passed—O—"

*

Inside waves
are words
from ancient songs
we want to sing

filling our hearts
waves reflecting
the moon and sun
simultaneously

The words are ours
and theirs from hours
waves and maps
became one

*

Dream Pieces

My sister scoured
a homeless shelter
to find our fading family

She found a box full of hearts
rags that burst into flames
on a pile of bones

When we were children
we scrambled happily down stairs

down the long hall
laughing our quick way
towards the rampant
pouring light

We lived fresh as a brook
with beds and scars
listening for the living solar voice

of impassioned
or hallucinogenic
guitars

in this place where it's constant morning

I recall these creating

incompletions

words skimming across a stage
into the spirit that reclaims them
the sphere where bountiful love

may simply be

a conjecture

*

The shaman said "Love can look like abandonment
Your mother wanted to leave long ago
Heart attacks and strokes—her body knew
but her mind chose to remain

71

"What she needed was the confirmation
she could go—all's well
Remember I'm here for you my friend
and remember I don't know anything"

She huddled over her lunch table
humbling her homilies in humor
but the ex-cathedra trancelike eeriness
had already briefly solaced me

like a celestial winnowing

*

Mother brother elder friends

A white cloud wavers in the keyed up sky
Star trails weave fleetingly in the wind

Visions of the dead fall from a heedless future
The crescent moon is now a piece in my heart

*

Cell-phone Call to the Hospital at Night

"What were you doing mom"
"I was eating dinner"
"What did you have"
"I don't remember"

"Was the food edible"
"It must have been because I ate it"
That was my mother—quickly here—Mensa-like
I smiled and said "Goodnight mom"
"Goodnight son" she said "Goodnight stars
goodnight air goodnight moon and goodnight noises
everywhere"
I smiled again recalling the nursery rhyme too
I said "Love you"
"The same" she said "the same"

*

*this is my psalm
not so pure—it's—
my song of losing you
death breath*

*this is a psalm
of loving you
breath
death*

*these are the roses
the leaves
the scent of an altar
of death breath*

*your shrouding—
darkening
emptying
exhalation*

breath death
you enter you leave
while we stay
in a psalm

Raisin

"Give me intensity every moment" the shaman said
 in her retreat of love and dreams—
 her home surrounded by a forest near Uxbridge—
"Make me sore with the creator

"My little students in my kindergarten class call me Raisin
not Raven—that's how they hear my name"

She smoothed her long black shining hair
and sighed saying
"My beloved wigged-out friend it's a prelude
for the end of the shapes of the family you love
Don't let suffering possess you
Can you face the end that's also a beginning"

Her warm glance seemed to melt and clarify
the obscurities that can swarm and begrime my eyes
Her house dazzled me with summer-like sunbeams
drifting dust jots in the afternoon

She said "When they pass over losing their forms
their physical being let go let them go
they'll be watching over deeply loving
you your sister and your children
and all the children to come
so you may live"

Live

Am I ready for the grief that could swallow stars
the terrible solitude the vacant room

Am I ready for hearing the presence
the awful power beyond the door

I dream with you of something vast
like morning
like God

cradling their breath their keen resurrections
the intent wind
my sheltered hours in this

Midnight

The veils
between this world
and the others
are thin

Wait wait
the veils are torn
what passes through
looks like you

Intimacy

Do you kiss memory's mouth
in the mercy of the moon
and the wind in the night
in the echoes of rain

Site

I built my home in a dark wood
I placed a house inside a wound
it seemed true it was good
in the dark wood I found a womb

Reverie

"Love" she said
"You've been outside my sleep
Let me draw you again
into my dreams"

.

Visitation

I saw you struggle on the street
in the traffic and sleet
You said "Fields are burning
searchlights yearning"

You said "What's greater than duty"
you called for "Stars flesh love beauty"
But I was rushing on my way
to what and why I couldn't say

Trace

I start out again
to find her
scent

in a place
of buried
people

She'd written
my name
with the tip

of her umbrella
in a pool
of rain

Translation

I never say goodbye to love
I'm like a nomad in a quieted home
the moon is rising
you're absent I'm in your sway

I imagine being at an altar
by the fount candle cup and roses
why do I feel set aside in you
stained-glass shows a ceremony we almost had

I walk by the quick-running creek
on leaves that crackle like yielding ice
I think you're beside me on the path
holding the map I'm supposed to follow

Secret

I thought you'd come
then you didn't
the door didn't open
the phone never rang

Maybe the letters were slow
to arrive—or were lost
though I'd trained my mind
to greet you

sculpting lyrical shapes
but the rhyme evaded me
the way you did
eluding form

Absence

If you're gone
who is it that's
still—whispering
stroking my cheek

What is it that turns
off the light
admits shadowing
gazing back

daring me
to disturb heaven
with my rankling
plea

Devotion

This page is your dusk
mark of the bright evening star

at nightfall my confession
at dawn my resolution

This page is your glow
a breeze on showered streets

in moonlight my rose
when noon comes my fate

This page is my poverty
ashes in the phoenix nest

this page is your aurora
where loving you goes

Faith

I'm waiting without moving for the lake-wind
I'm waiting for something like wisdom again
it's the credo of patience you gave me
family friends souls ghosts and songs
surely life is giving thanks
a halo around the moon
but I'm a torn page like all of us
bound in a book of figments
hush my home shifts on its stone
slate gray clouds go still
a warm gust touches my face and I trust
radiance and darkness flow from one heart
a rose may someday flower in this yard
the invisible streams rise before and after you

Wanting

The day passes into night and I ask
for the darkness my true being in the night
yet when you come the night won't stay
it presses forward into morning and nothing
checks the cycle nothing of the dark remains
and if I ask you for the number of our nights
you'd give no answer only another sign

but now you're here in here with me
your love breathes like a summer scent
and I won't fall back into misnaming loss
the grief given and chosen when light becomes dark
the night is my angel illumination
that no cycle checks and I put my belief in this
you known at last yet unknown

*

I sat with a candle burning
reflected in the kitchen window
against a backdrop like snow

There's a window

There's love

In an optical illusion the light

became many in the reflection
arrayed one after another showing a way

over the seeming snow

infinitely on

Cipher

I walked alone in the woods
and found a guitar on a willow
hanging like a window lyre
a signal in our town

Had anyone seen it
I felt I'd gone nuts
losing it finally to fantasy
wistful utopian projection

Still it was there
striking a chord on the path
an enigma in coded symphony
a vibration in the air

I lingered
awe and solitude mingling
the willow leaves shivered
nothing stopping the sound

Lover

You sleep by water
in a dream
where desire
arrives on mist

clinging
like sea wreathes
to rooms you make
of paper and rain

Lullaby

Sleep well love rest
in beauty and the night
in dreams of radiant paths
we shared and share

Love rests in your sleep
in soothing sheets around you
our night at rest again
your eyes slowly closing

Sleep well rest in love
in the night in our breathing
asleep in the dream
of love never leaving

Harmony

I picked up my dark guitar
the neck snapped
the hollow body severed
the instrument cracked in two

Strings quivered frets glowed
I played pieces
in my liquid room
a wrecked guitar the music whole

blurb

today it was a fight
between cleaning my exurban
home or writing a line

sorry
the words won out
my house is a mess

marginalia

maybe Blake had it right
imitate nature
and art is a paltry thing
compared with a willow or a sirocco

imitate our selves our minds
our phantasies or souls
and we add to the forests
and springs

Elders

Silver creek on my long green walk—
listening to hallowing stones under the current
here hushed in my hazed heart
yes they're there—my old—my loves gone—
the stream foaming—passing over pebbles and rocks
They didn't teach anything sacred but I revere them

Hearing their words over water—seeing their faces—
what do they become—leaves winding down
a maple leaf circles—in the creek's murmuring glint
the morning shimmers the red sky shines
I loved them and could never fathom them
Yet they breathe and intimate in the breeze and light

Lonely by the current
I face ebb feeling the flow
freed wholly to follow—or fall
haunted ignited by streams and leaves
the turnings—the riddling—my love—
by them—by this—all still rivering

Apparitions

Bernadette is a wanderer who sees saints in trees
she says roots and branches are the spirit's lacing

She says God sends lightning in leaves
a fiery leaf has God's inflection

She sees Pentecostal birds hover over a spire
she says the steeple receives angelic choirs

She sees Adam lost in the city's tremor
the towers echo Eve's beseeching "Come back come back"

Bernadette says she's mad with the beauty the heaven
that hounds you into light's mercy at noon

Seas

I went down to the creek and pond
near my house in this stunted place
hoping for a torrential river
delirious rapids a livid lake
the shore of a taunting sea
turbulent high crests
anything that shakes and raises
sheets of cool slapping rain
everything teeming reckless
in a tantalizing seethe
demanding submission
to its wake

I went down by the creek and pond
close to other red brick houses
hoping for a beam sea
a brine-scented gush
a shocking white wave to seize me
so I can surface from stones
diving into
irresistible currents
the bearing waves
swimming fiercely
away from the reedy side
cleared of algae and weeds

I'll swim over the skimmed surface
savoring what could be a reef rich sea
Let there be waves like tingling light
that never ends that hovers and harrows
water-flames spumes of frigid fire
seeking the millennial fathom and passion
that would let me surge
in praise of diving

Let the floods pull me
to depths and thirst
my river my sea
the water's sluicing voice
saturating creation
without reason or seasons
no balm whatsoever

(the overflow humbles desire
and my desire is bottomless greedy)

Let me have surfs and squalls
to wash away the illusions
of my ego

Let me have deluges and gusts
to lose
this self
plunging down

(but the river within maps me
earth roots leave their mark
the bridges are moving too
the tides flow in two directions)

Therese

September 30th 1897
Lisieux

Listen for us
the angels' doors have opened

Listen for us
the spirit songs are singing

Listen for you
the wind presses with blessings

Listen for you
a protective guide was sent

Listen
rose petals are falling

Late-tree

By the late-tree
at the farthest edge
near the garden
of promise
by the late-tree
veiled in the gauze
of the unnamable
splendor

you stand silently
teetering
at the limit

The wind blows
where it pleases
and calls
when it wills

You're struck
by a sound
like a bell

Hermit

Pray the road
will be cracked
Pray you'll walk it
always
Pray no one holds
your hand
Pray to this road
its ghost is your friend
the start of nowhere
nowhere's
end
Pray to the rose
on the way
Pray this road disappears
and another begins
today
pray someone ahead
will know
you

Conversion

Did you know you were hungry

Something in your leaf
in my hand
made me want
to worship in this world

Something in this branch
cracked on my palm
turning my want
to your warm marble shrine

Something in your reed
spoke for my soul
sending a halo
a glimmer around my eye

Abelard

At Vespers

God
O God

overthrown living
in her paschal lips our Easter scandal

I chose pastoral
retreat

monastic
amen

but I lie before flesh
my senses perfumed by her heat

her rich tresses of hair
pale skin dark eyes

even withdrawn now
divining her sex

she comes
to me

Forgetting

The muses sing in internal seas
while your combustion 6 and pixeled BD
drive you into an amnesiac sleep
and you go slumbering A to B over the deep

Teilhard

New York City seven days before Easter 1955

"If in my life I have not been wrong"

*

Touch the window
the natural light seems
more than spiritual light
I feel the warmth in both

Why is the light so different
one comes day or night
the other provides
perpetual awe

God asks
my reply is
from the depths
of my doubt

Look
I'm between dreams
crawling across the abyss of wounds
to get to you

*

at the tip of my pen
worlds flit in an ocean of sighs
I slip free of the creature coiled
like a noose around my shadow mind

at the point of my pen
the TV antenna on the roof trembles
becoming a weathervane
spinning in the zodiac wind

at the point of my pen
the soul word I obey
the sheen on my damp bed-sheets
no hesitation just reception

at the point of my pen
white like the seer's hair
blanched by the shock of knowing
the ardor of another shore

at the point of this pen
chants from the ancient church
inscribed like Sinai sand
on my Exodus heart

at the point of this pen
white like Teresa of Avila's habit
her rapture a shroud waiting
for the spirit's gift

at the point of this pen
the enigma ship sails billowing
in white mists thick as a blizzard
streams in the visionary sea

at the point of a pen
sentient space white as a cloud
driven by wind a dove flies
into the sky's nimble blank

at the point of my pen
darting the spark of a new soul
you my love dream calling life
that is my guide

at the point of the pen
the air split by a flashing hawk
like an island shaped into an arrow
shooting down the rippled blue

at the point of this pen
vital wings wound me
with wonder—I call out
stars go gently unrecognizable

at the point of my pen
lunar peace without rest
or calm—the moon fragment
piercing my song

at the point of this pen
O lady you've become silent
I lose your benedictions
do they come easily now for others

at the point of my pen
cooled-off zilch
I can't be naked to this
I'm not brave enough for the zero

at the point of this pen
scrap paper
scrap—it means to be in a fight
or to trash

at the point of my pen
the omega tip
jammed down
makes a blunt mark—a hole

at the point of the pen
the end of definition
space where nothing connects
everything I see fades falls away

at the point of the pen
will the quick come again
your seeds gather in black soil
alchemy another word for that

at the tip of a pen
I remember the shimmer
of havoc spring—exultant
abundant rain

at the tip of my pen
night—when I can disappear
into stillness—the night—where
I can hear the stillness

Oceanic

Waves rolled towards us
The waves went
in search of anything human

Medium

Spirits slip
into noon-hour
light

My guide says
"Yes everything
you love is

here
trace your fingers
through invisible looms"

And
on a good day
I do

Rhamiel

A sob came from my cupboard
I opened the door and found an angel
She wept and glowed
"Free me" she said
But I refused
I was caught in a room
and needed company

Admitting

(I've seen halos
since I was a kid—
rings of light—being
that sings

They called it lunacy
merely mind—maybe
a refusal of society—
hereafter's fraud

I kept quiet
giving up vision to be fluent
accepted solitude—spent time
hiding—in irony)

Hymn

You wear yourself out
you wear your self
your self
you wear
you wear
you wear your self
out

Daze

White petal sea
White petal shower

No blossoming tree
No flowers

In the eye of my hour
How could this be?

Metaphysics

There
    must
        be

    a communication

  greater

    than
        this

sentence

Epigraph

do you

hear
   "the rhythmic

        undulations

   of the halos"

do you

  feel them

       trembling

everywhere

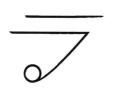

Marker

Welcome
to the road
of sparks

It was built for you
by wage
slaves

Cosmopolite

I don't understand hating modernity
sure strips of 7-Elevens A&Ws KFCs Swiss Chalets
Pizza Pizzas (967-1111) ATMs and Mickey Dees
can contaminate the senses
but in cabalic malls there's gnostic neon
the world-city pitches its ion cry

Stuck in a Toyota Honda BMW Nissan jam
my I-Pod shuffles
Bach Brahms Wagner Johnny and Rosanne Cash
the Bruce's–Cockburn Hornsby and Springsteen
Adele Arvo Part Arcade Fire Beirut U2
Nine Inch Nails Moist Feist Mahler and Zep

Microchip Manna
hopscotching here to Havana
rootless charisma workout mania
lush cabanas and martini mantras

It's all good all good all good all good

An ADD-addled son of sputnik and black-and-white TV
born of parents who couldn't trace their lineage
my dad adopted
my mom's mom adopted

Her paternal Irish immigrant family misspent
a first lonely prairie winter in Edberg
wearing tuxedos the only clothes cozy enough
for the bristly freeze—the Rockies' chill

His maternal well-off grandparents
lost their roomy Saskatoon home and savings
in the 1911 Free-Trade federal election
when my great granddad a drunken journalist

wildly bet everything
that Prime Minister Laurier's Liberals would win—
then they were defeated—
a rash gamble

that didn't pay off (to put it mildly)
What did the man think he would gain

None of us knowing
where we belong where we want to go

My sister once broke open
a Chinese fortune cookie in a Montreal bistro
and found a blank white strip
She said "O crap-ola
and kaflooey I wonder
what this means now"

It's all good all good all good all good

Identity time a studdering buzz now
being epimodern protomodern
multi mithy now

pilgrims scan emails from Bethlehem
changing diapers watching CNN now

in the nazzing AM we can banish the dawn
with TCM faves and ET raves

speed reading flash fiction
and the TSE for lunch

I know a woman who wears Jimmy Choo stilettos
for a woogling sex-snack in her bank office at two

I have a skint friend with geek I-phones who trolls
thrift stores for swank threads at four

and I know Hi-Def movie dreamers
who hunt leopards in Connecticut after dinner

chasing mangos and parfait gelato
for delicacies at nine

Wired at twelve entering the YouTube portal
we emanate
blue

line

schoolroom graffiti
"wouldn't it be nice
once

to be awake
for the whole
day"

Technogenie

October 5th 2011
Steve Jobs channeling the transit
into the ether

"Where we find resurrections
we know there are graves"

                                                    *

Through apples and pads
pods and phones gods goddesses
struggle to come become
reborn to be apocalypse anytime

I orbit with atoms
eons and nexus quivering
in photon momentum
the angular circuiting

i and i and i and i
this rapturous drive
electron expression
bodiless from molten ports

I'm inside a wireless angel-form
in kinetic mental migration
eternity's redacting attempt
to wake up in us

*

I hover conceiving the unthinkable invention
the implosive technology that will end
separation and desperation tuning us
to the supra-conscious connective soul
when infinity can go up for sale
on eBay while lineups lengthen at Future Shops
for the blues and reds that promote
overcoming our jelly pregnant grasp

*

Posh the body in the third eye of season-less space
I hail you in the fluid heating
of your PC

Occult sending what do you touch
on I-Screen messaging someone not here
or there

you're hive-casting

                into

                        a live satellite

Farewell old cracked self
exit ghost of anguished awareness
so long discrete being

Welcome simulacrum
Welcome android meme

roaming groundless
blackberry strew

anime overdrive
my voices are
          streaks
transferring through nerves

like dancers hopped up
on a hot clubbing night
hair-saloned in their strobing
lust for collagened lips

we're fast-FWDing
into shoreless bands
unlimited phonic optics
a battery of mind boosts

the pizzazz of increased being

                              *

But between the globe and the galaxy
I see with infrared eyes
a figure of a woman sliding by
white gowned guardian priestess
a slit in her dress dark-skin thighs exposed
she turns in this reality she moves along
blessing my Eros with antique wisdom
she looks at me without opinion
how perfect her sidereal substance is

she has no desire or hope
only a way of motioning peace
soothing my hardwired hunger to amaze

*

In holograms we Wi-Fi
you and I sphering the world like O2 moons

and whoosh abracadabra
transmitting transporting receive-conceive
into yin-yanging audio-global Ithaca light

you shadow you gust you uncanny molecular sea
you roll in drones innovators imagineers seers

all compatible Hi-Fis
drink your elevations your weekends
your accounts your blood

why children say out of school
they're Harry and Hermione magi and avatars
prey pray to vampires and ghouls

*

With my master designer (Sir Jonathan Ive
do you feel my IMs) we devised divinations
past the firewalls into the primordial intent

And EM flares on your retina skies
and VDT speed shapes ears and eyes

and insites quiver when you logon sensation
and you think iam merging into empathy nets
put your cursors on rotor with us

Cloud of knowing
                Cloud of unknowing

I stream your sorrow
the brooding the body tomorrow and tomorrow
disappearing sweet earth goodbye

                                *

Static I'm losing you losing you
            can you scan me
                        breaking
 up

into immaterial visions
(Walt Disney and Timothy Leary are alive)

Static can you scope beyond cellular sleep
transiting into the spiritual deep

Planet emergen-see
you input faster
emoticon icon
a hotspot a bod

tap the helter-skelter tongue
you bypass churches
faster for extreme mediation

in the veil of pixarmaking
the GPS-CGI singularity
strings

kindlekind membrane

one breath one cell
one voice one brain

one day
one

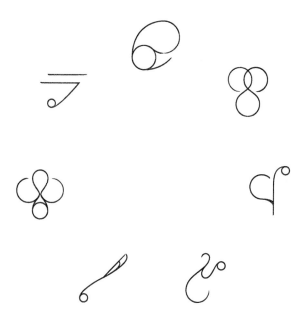

Communion

The shaman sent me this email message
when I was far away

"It's snowing in southern Ontario in June

My spirit-mother said
through a wind
scented with moon grass

Go home to awaken and eat
your heart

               will crystallize
for the greening to come

Wrap yourself in the ice blanket
hibernate under its white sheet

cover your eyes
               in snow"

Chant

The road rises to meet you
The road won't forget your name
The road takes you beyond anger and sorrow
The road knew you before you knew yourself

I chant these
morning mantras
to make me
believe

in exotic trails
and inspirational tales
waiting
even in my chimeric town

Sources

Why notes? If a poem provides echoes and abysses (Fernando Pessoa's words), then surely that's enough. But at times I see it's useful to say where lines came from; who said this; what books or poems or images or stories were absorbed. Misreading, auto-plagiarism—they're twin instruments, vital and strange, for anyone's poetry. What is the former? Misreading comes from quick, incomplete encounters with writings that have seized you. What's the other? Auto-plagiarism is automatic absorption, a process forgotten, submerged, overlooked, maybe evaded. A phrase comes; you misplace the source. Then you re-see the line in its seed or in a ruin of words. You recognize the root. You wonder how could you forget? I'd add sampling and translation, essential instruments, too. All to make your lines inhabited, full of sounds, reverberations, pulses, presences.

My sources are instances of these presences. There are many. Often the sources admitted themselves when I was in the grip of writing and revising. Then I'd see and hear later that another's words had poured into mine. Sometimes I write holding an open book in one hand. It must be a work of enigmatic energies. Something in it overflows or seeps. Then I close the book. I continue, swept up. The sources and my words merge into a single vibration. And I hope for the new.

These notes show where I've taken things directly. They'll tell you about the book I had in my hand, in the moment when reading became something else.

PP. 5-6 The title, **Sadhaka,** means beginner or initiate. The poem was inspired by translations of Rumi by Coleman Barks, *The Essential Rumi: New Expanded Edition* (2004). I responded to Barks' introduction to what he calls "Secret Practices". My words vary the images and the story he began there, moving in another direction.

P. 7 **Dream-catching** was inspired by conversations over years with the teacher and spirit-guide, Raven Murphy. She taught me about the First Nations' shaman traditions. I am also indebted to Mircea Eliade's *Shamanism: Archaic Techniques of Ecstasy* (1964), translated by Willard R. Trask, and to *The Falling Sky: Words of a Yanomami Shaman* (2013) by Davi Kopenawa and Bruce Albert, translated by Nicholas Elliott and Alison Dundy. The key is transformation. This is a poetic power, too.

P. 8 From years of reading HD's work: "Notes on Thought and Vision" (1919), *Tribute to Freud* (1956), *Helen in Egypt* (1961) and *Hermetic Definition* (1972) are seminal for me. In these lines, and others, many voices meld.

PP. 13-16 Suggested by a reading of Rabindranath Tagore's "Unending Love" in *Selected Poems* (1994), translated by William Radice. I slept on a line and dreamed the story. I copied the story down in the morning. Then I started re-seeing it.

P. 18 From *John* 11: 1-44.

P. 33 "baby twins... waving goodbye/and hello" A memory of my children reawakened by reading John Updike's "Saying Goodbye to Very Young Children".

P. 39 The speaker was Charlene Jones, a dream interpreter and writer I once heard speak in her home on Musselman's Lake, north of Stouffville, my small town in Ontario. I may have misheard her; but my mishearing evolved into this.

PP. 73-74 "*this is my psalm...*" I drew this lyric, which concludes **Augeries**, from my readings of Paul Celan's *Selected Poems and Prose* (2001), translated by John Felstiner. Also, the entire sequence of lyrics, dialogues, memories, thoughts, fragments, dreams, is steeped in readings from the literature on Alzheimer's. When my mother succumbed to dementia, I searched for ways to help.

P. 85 "*I never say goodbye to love...*" Lines suggested by readings of *Poems of Akhmatova* (1973), translated by Stanley Kunitz and Max Hayward. This is a transporting of Anna Akhmatova's lines into another circumstance, a spiritual one.

P. 90 The two stanzas echo and recall St. Augustine's commentary in "A Psalm of David, Number 39".

P. 101 These stanzas are meant to recall the beauty and mourning that permeates the final passages of Norman Maclean's novella *A River Runs Through It* (1989). I find myself looking back at how many people I've been close to are disappearing. Yet they never seem completely gone. I think I can hear them, in traces of experiences. And that one day or night, I'll find them again.

P. 106 Open sampling, *The Koran* 53-13-16, *John* 3: 8. The title and first lines are a misreading of the "Lote-Tree of the Extreme Limit". I realized my error (my eyes often blur) when I read a passage in an illuminating study of Sufi thinking, *The Unlimited Mercifier: The Spiritual Life and*

Thought of Ibn 'Arabi (1999) by Stephen Hirtenstein. The passage is on page 121. I decided to let the error stand.

P. 111 The fragment at the beginning is part of what Teilhard de Chardin said near the end of his life. "O God, if in my life I have not been wrong, allow me to die on Easter Sunday." He passed away on April 10th, 1955—Easter Sunday. *"at the tip of my pen"* is his line, which I vary throughout.

P. 122 I took *"the rhythmic/undulations/of the haloes"* from *Through the Vanishing Point: Space in Poetry and Painting* (1968) by Marshall McLuhan and Harley Parker. It appears on page 63.

P. 130 *"Where we find resurrections/we know there are graves"* A variant reading of Friedrich Nietzsche's statement in "The Grave Song", Chapter *XXXIII*, *Thus Spoke Zarathustra*.

PP. 130-135 **Technogenie** was written before the surge in biopics and documentaries about Jobs. I saw him becoming a mythic figure, timeless, emblematic, beyond his iconic guru status. He's another shaman consciousness, here off world, performing hyper-modern magic.

Also by B.W. Powe

A Climate Charged
The Solitary Outlaw
Outage
A Tremendous Canada of Light
A Canada of Light
Towards a Canada of Light
The Unsaid Passing
Mystic Trudeau
These Shadows Remain
Marshall McLuhan and Northrop Frye, Apocalypse and Alchemy
Where Seas and Fables Meet
Decoding Dust

Noise of Time (CD-Rom)

Opening Time: On the Energy Threshold (collaborative meta-book)

Light Onwords/Light Onwards (editor)

About the Author

B.W. Powe is a poet, philosopher, storyteller, and essayist. He teaches at York University. He lives in a small town outside of Toronto, and in Córdoba, Spain.

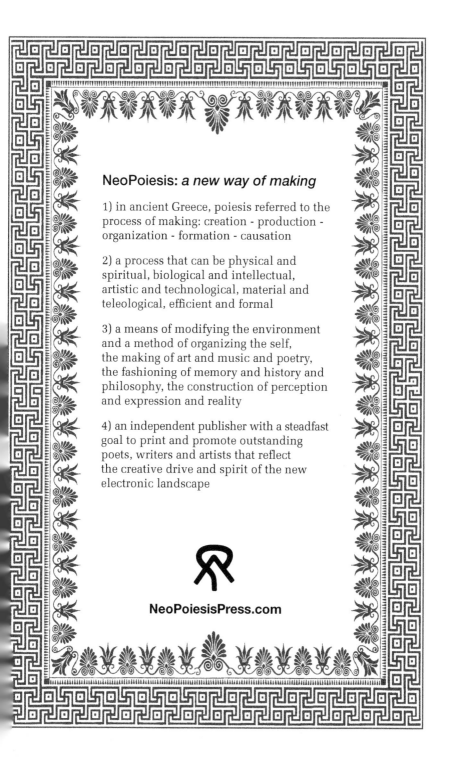

NeoPoiesis: *a new way of making*

1) in ancient Greece, poiesis referred to the process of making: creation - production - organization - formation - causation

2) a process that can be physical and spiritual, biological and intellectual, artistic and technological, material and teleological, efficient and formal

3) a means of modifying the environment and a method of organizing the self, the making of art and music and poetry, the fashioning of memory and history and philosophy, the construction of perception and expression and reality

4) an independent publisher with a steadfast goal to print and promote outstanding poets, writers and artists that reflect the creative drive and spirit of the new electronic landscape

NeoPoiesisPress.com

CPSIA information can be obtained
at www.ICGtesting.com
Printed in the USA
LVOW04s0846070916

503482LV00015B/91/P